Reflections In Recovery

Reflections In Recovery

✦

The Attributes of Being Average

Ed W. Houston

iUniverse, Inc.

New York Lincoln Shanghai

Reflections In Recovery
The Attributes of Being Average

iUniverse books may be ordered through booksellers or by contacting:

iUniverse
2021 Pine Lake Road, Suite 100
Lincoln, NE 68512
www.iuniverse.com
1-800-Authors (1-800-288-4677)

ISBN-13: 978-0-595-39641-2 (pbk)
ISBN-13: 978-0-595-84044-1 (ebk)
ISBN-10: 0-595-39641-0 (pbk)
ISBN-10: 0-595-84044-2 (ebk)

Printed in the United States of America

Contents

1

Reflections in Recovery

Hi, my name is Ed.

Up until a few years ago, I was just your average, run-of-the-mill, everyday dope addict. You know the kind. The kind that wakes up every morning with an equal need for air and dope; believing both are necessary for life. The kind of dope fiend that has only one rule: get the dope, no matter what, by any means necessary, easy or hard.

Everything, and I mean everything, revolved around this rule.

It didn't start out that way, but by the end drugs and alcohol had become the focal point of my whole existence. I've since learned that alcohol is considered a drug in most Anonymous circles. After all, it is a mind-altering chemical.

Looking back with hindsight, that most excellent form of vision, I see that given my emotional and mental makeup, I didn't have a chance.

I was an easy mark, a patsy, a chump, a trick, a sucker, an all-day lollipop, and eventually a whore being worked by the most ruthless pimp in the game, one who never takes "no" or "I can't" for an answer when you work for him.

I guess it's safe to say that I started out like everybody else, in the sense that I was born human. In that respect we're all alike, but that's where the similarity ends. While we're all alike, each one of us is different—we have different shapes, sizes, and colors. We're also different with respect to age and sex, and we speak different languages and dialects. All of these differences are physical and very superficial in the larger scheme of things. What really makes us different is how we think, perceive, and react toward external stimuli (life).

From babyhood on, all of us are exposed to different sights, sounds, words, emotions, and actions from others—from actions that seemingly have no impact to ones that affect our behavior for years to come. Some of us can be exposed to the same external events yet react totally differently. We perceive differently. We react differently. In that regard, we're the same.

Since all of us are different, we need guidelines to make living together tolerable for all of us, or rather the majority. This is what we call "society." Boundaries are determined, and when crossed, penalties are imposed on those who cross them; these boundaries are called laws. The majority of society abides by these guidelines and stays within the boundaries they have set up as laws.

The majority also sets up boundaries of correct social behavior. For example, it's okay to drink, but not to get drunk. Or, it's all right to chew food, but not with your mouth open. Or, it's okay to disagree, but not to make a scene in public. That sort of correct social behavior. Alcoholics and addicts almost always go beyond the guidelines society has set, and they do break the law; that's usually a certainty. Those of us who are alcoholics and addicts usually stretch past the limits of socially acceptable behavior time and time again before we finally do break the law.

I've stated that all of us are different. Alcoholics and addicts are different in that our perceptions and reactions to external stimuli (life) drive us to share the same experience to alcohol and drugs. That reaction/experience is abuse of and a craving for our drug of choice, a choice that can end with us in jail or some likewise confining institution. The choice may even lead to the ultimate confinement, the grave. That is, unless we can find relief from our plight, with the help of others like ourselves, through a power greater than ourselves.

This story and the accompanying poetry is how I found that power greater than me.

Once again, using the clearest form of vision, hindsight, I see that early in my life slight deviations from accepted social behaviors would take me on a journey that would last over thirty years. It was a journey that, progressively with each step, transformed me into a social vampire, a vampire that would feed off anything or anybody around me to get my fix.

I didn't understand why I couldn't do like or be like everyone else who could have a few drinks or take a few puffs off the old weed and still operate within the boundaries of what the majority considered normal. It wasn't until I got into a twelve-step program and began to understand and accept what I was, and why I did what I did, that I realized what a little deviation, if left unchecked, could develop into. Left unchecked, I reaped what I sowed.

2

Pitfalls of Deviation

The word "deviant" means a person who deviates from what is considered normal in a group or society. So, a deviant is a person who deviates.

Webster's says that when a person deviates, they turn aside from a course, direction, or standard doctrine. Another definition of deviate suggests a turning aside, often to only a slight degree, from the correct or prescribed course.

"Swerve" is a synonym for deviate, implying a sudden or sharp turning from a path or course. Deviation can then be thought of in terms of degrees, from turning aside slightly to a sudden or sharp turning away from a previously accepted action.

What was my degree of deviation? Did I deviate a little or a lot? Under what circumstances did I deviate?

In the society I live in, the norm is to abstain from drugs and not to get drunk on alcohol. That's normal. At first, I just slightly turned away from this accepted commandment of society. A beer here and there, a little weed, but just on the weekends, buzzed but not drunk, a little high but not stoned.

I was just slightly deviating from the norm, just a little—not hurting anyone, not causing any trouble. Hell, it's not like I was robbing or stealing (yet).

What's the big deal?

The big deal, which I didn't know at the time, was that a progressive disease, if left unchecked, would become worse and worse.

What disease?

I was young.

I was smart.

I was strong.

I was just getting high on the weekends and one or two times during the week. Getting high couldn't stop me. I was going places in life. The only thing I'd ever be hooked on was money and women, exactly in that order. Didn't everybody call me E.C. (Eddie Cool)? This was a new day and a new time—the mid-1970s, the Age of Aquarius, Free Love, and Flower Power. I could control my getting high.

Cunning, baffling, and progressive, my slight deviations began to increase by degrees in frequency, duration, and potency. Imported beers, wines with maturity, and liqueurs of fine spirits became my drinks of choice. Hash oil, Thai stick, and Kona Gold became the smoke of a connoisseur.

I had a good job, and I deserved a drink of the good stuff and a little smoke when I came home from a hard day's work. Besides, what would the girlies say if E.C. didn't have the best stuff to "git high."

Looking back now, yeah, I was young and strong, but there was nothing smart about not looking past the flash that glittered but was not gold. The bigger a young man's ego (or any man's ego, for that matter) is, the less he can really see what's real around him. The larger the ego, the less able he is to see beyond the self. The only matters in life become self-matters.

Cunning, baffling, progressive...I didn't know I had a disease, but I sensed something was wrong. The cunningness of my disease also sensed that I might be becoming aware I had a problem. Like a dictator trying to smash a small resistance before it can become a revolution, my addiction escalated in frequency and power.

At about the same time, red devils (sleeping pills under the brand name Seconal) hit the scene. They were also known as "stums," because of the stumbling behavior you would exhibit after they dissolved inside you, and "fender benders," because trying to operate a car after taking some would at least guarantee you a dented fender if not a total wreck.

With the introduction of red devils in my life, my disease laid the foundation for my eventual trip to the Land of Nod.

There were three modes of addiction for me—speed, mellow, and downers. Most people who get high eventually try all three. Some like the speed with the methamphetamine and the cocaine. Some like the mellow with the chronic (marijuana), alcohol, wine, and beer. Some like the down-side, with the barbiturates and the king. The King is also known as smack, 11-500, Do J, black tar, Mexican mud, and China white, but he's the King, King Heroin.

He's a two-faced king who shows a benevolent, kind, caring face to all beginners who wish to put all their cares upon him. He will gently take all your cares and worries, telling you everything will be all right, as he lulls you to sleep. Again and again, you go to your benevolent sovereign with every problem, with every worry. He'll make you forget your problems, as he transports you to the Land of Nod (the euphoric semi-sleep state induced by heroin).

The Land of Nod, where every inhabitant is guaranteed not to have a care in the world. A domain where problems cease to exist, where responsibility to mother, father, sister, brother, wife, husband, boyfriend, girlfriend, child, and employer is banned by royal edict of the King, for all allegiance must be to the King.

Cunning, baffling...too late did I learn of the enemy within, who lived to destroy the house in which it dwelt. When red devils were released into my bloodstream, defiance, arrogance, and power coursed through my veins. None could defy Eddie Cool.

This feeling was short lived, only about thirty minutes. After that, I would either pass out or be too loaded to know what I was doing. During the short span of those thirty minutes, the deviant was let loose to do what deviants do best, turn away from the norm, slightly or sharply. Black eyes, bloody noses, broken bones, and other fighting trophies, some of which I received but most of which I bestowed upon others. Mayhem and even near-death resulted from these incidents, which invariably led me to swear off red devils.

The violence reds invoked in me could no longer be tolerated. I knew I had to stop taking them. I knew that was the right course of action, but I missed the sensation of the reds bursting, dissolving inside me. Was there any way to experience the sensation and power without the violence?

Cunning, baffling, powerful...my deviation was almost ninety degrees from the norm.

Not able to hold a job for any length of time—too much absenteeism and tardiness. It was always their fault, not mine because I would drink, get high, and stay up all night.

Problems with my woman. Hell, I was grown, past twenty-one! I didn't have to tell any woman where I was going or when I was coming. It wasn't any of her damned business what I did with my money. Who did she think she was?

My parents were complaining that I hadn't paid them the last money I had already borrowed from them, and now I was trying to borrow some more. My sisters and brother were always trying to stick their noses in my business. Something was always going wrong, bullshit in the air everywhere. Weed, booze, and cocaine just didn't hit the spot. Sometimes, I wished I could scream myself into oblivion.

Cunning, baffling, powerful...my disease made a way for me to solve my problems. I had a good friend, whom I now understand (in hindsight) was a deviant just like me, except he was a few degrees further along from the norm than me. My friend and I were of the same polarity. Unlike a magnet, in which opposite poles attract, we were drawn together in our deviation. My friend brought me to the throne of the King. I was told that the King had the power to heal all my wounds and make the problems go away, and he did. The King let me into his kingdom, the Land of Nod. I didn't want to stay in the Land of Reality.

There, I was a deviant.

I always turned aside from the norm, whether slightly or sharply. I didn't know why. Something was wrong with me. I was abnormal. I couldn't be like everybody else. I was a deviant and I didn't want to think about it, and I didn't have to in the Land of Nod.

Cunning, baffling, and now with a treaty with the King, my disease is now extremely powerful.

At first I went and visited the King once a day, and he would let me stay in his kingdom all day long. I didn't have a care in the world and I felt no pain, no pain, no-o-o-o pain.

Of course, I'd have to come back to the Land of Reality and become that deviant again, deviating in society to make my trips to see the King, but just slightly. My trips weren't that much, just $10 a day. Ten dollars was nothing for a stepper like me. Things were beginning to look good again.

I liked the King. He was so good and understanding. He filled me. He was better than anything, and when he was with his Queen (cocaine), their offspring, the speedball, was everything.

Cunning, baffling, progressive.

Needless to say, I began to visit the King twice a day. I couldn't stay in the Land of Nod as long as I used to. I had to come back and be that deviant. So I deviated more and more, taking more and more trips to see the King. Three times a day. Four times a day. Five times a day. All day, every day.

Less and less, I got to stay in the Land of Nod. More and more, I had to stay in the Land of Reality and be that deviant. But that deviant was the one I was trying to get away from in the first place.

Finally, the day came when the King said, "You can no longer come to the Land of Nod, but you must still pay for the trip."

"Hell No! If I can't get to nod, I'm not going to pay."

Just then the King's head spun around—the face was ugly, the eyes glaring with hate. The King spoke. "Oh yes! You will pay and you will pay every day, all day, and you will not be late. You will start early every morning, and you will pay late into the night. You see, I have another place you've never been before. It's called the House of Pain, and if you don't pay you'll be there every day. It's just the place for deviants like you. So get back to reality, for you and the Land of Nod are through."

My tolerance to heroin had become so high that my daily doses no longer got me high. Now the heroin only kept me from experiencing painful withdrawal symptoms. If I didn't take my regular shots of heroin throughout the day, I would become physically ill, with extreme nausea, cramping, diarrhea, fever, and chills. The groovy, good, get-high feeling of heroin was finished in my life. The King had showed his true face. Heroin had become elevated to its rightful position in my life, right alongside air. I needed both to live.

Cunning, baffling, powerful...

This writing assignment ("Pitfalls of Deviation") was to be a punishment for a slight infraction, a small deviation from one of the rules at the Wayback Inn (my last rehabilitation center, in 1994). I started out writing this assignment with the idea that I, Me, Self, would show the counselors at the Wayback Inn how stupid this slight turning away from a prescribed course of action really was. What I wound up with was a look at how slight deviations in the early part of my life led to deeper deviations, becoming more progressive and pronounced as my life made the slow slide into the pit in which all addicts and alcoholics sooner or later find themselves.

I operated from a self-created pit of despair; despair formed by the negative residue of circumstances generated by me in my quest to quench the unquenchable. Sitting here in the Wayback Inn, finishing this assignment, I realized that the Enemy had fed me the Okie-Doke, and I had bitten hook, line, and sinker. I had swallowed the lie. I actually believed I was different from most people in my circle. I believed I was the Master of my drugs, not the other way around. That's why I found myself one more morning, before I entered the Wayback Inn, waiting for the bus to go buy some dope.

3

Business as Usual

I had already started my daylong ritual well before daybreak. You see, contrary to popular belief, most hardcore addicts are very early risers. That's when we catch most of you (the general public) slipping, or with your guard down, and then we stick it to you.

The previous night I spotted an open field in an industrial area that was being corralled with new sheets of tin. All they had was a lock and no dogs. Can you believe it? They wanted someone to have it; might as well be me. In the wee hours of the morning, I came and took their fence down. I loaded it on a grocery basket—the police had already taken two vans and two cars from me because of tickets, tags, and crimes (proven or suspected) committed with my vehicle—and pushed it two miles to a fence (a buyer of stolen goods) that dealt in that type of merchandise, all before 6:30 in the morning. No job is too big or too small for your properly motivated addict.

As I was waiting for the bus to take me to get my morning dose of medicine (heroin), I saw a lady talking to all the people waiting for the bus, steadily working herself up towards me.

Damn! I thought. *Damn! Where's the bus?* I wished it would get here before the old lady could get to me. I could see she was carrying a big Bible in her hands, and I just knew she was singling me out.

Shit, hurry up, bus! I said to myself as I looked up the street in the direction the bus would come.

I felt her standing up over me even before I looked back and up into her face. I was ready for her.

"How are you today, young man? And God bless you," she said.

"I'm fine, thank you. What about you?"

"I'm blessed, and do you know that God loves you?" she said.

"Yeah, I've been told that before."

"Son, Hell is a real place, a terrible place, more frightening than anyone alive can imagine. If you don't accept Jesus Christ into your life as your savior and repent, that's where you'll spend eternity."

Boy, was I ready for her. I let loose the first barrage. Standing up and shouting at her, I said, "Look, lady, I've known about Jesus and the church all my life, but knowing about it didn't keep me away from this!"

I went into my coat pocket and came out with my metal/antenna straight shooter (cocaine pipe) and shoved it in front of her face.

Then I let go the second barrage (pow!), still shouting, "Or this…"

I went to my inside coat pocket and came out with my syringe and cooker (heroin paraphernalia), pushing them up under her nose.

Now for the one-two punch: "Or these…"

I pulled up both sleeves of my coat, showing her the trails twenty-five years of needle marks had made over both arms.

"Yeah," I hollered at her, "I know I'm going to Hell."

Now I was grinning, because I knew by the shock on her face that I had taken some of the wind out of her sails. I circled the bus bench and moved toward her.

As she backed up, I continued.

"Hell!" I shouted. "I'm living in hell right now. The only wake-up from this zombie life I see is death!"

Then, acknowledging it to myself as much as I was saying it to her, I realized some wind had been taken out of my own sails.

I said to her more calmly, "Lady, I'm hooked, and the hook is in twenty years deep. It's over for me. I'll never be free. It's been so long, I don't remember what right is—and what's worse, I don't want to. Lady, I know you mean well and what you have to share is valid, but I'm beyond anything you could offer. Now, no disrespect, ma'am, but miss me with that shit you're trying to deliver. I've got real issues to deal with, like when is the motha-fuckin bus going to get here so I can cop my morning wakeup."

As I said this, I looked the old lady in the eye. I wasn't necessarily mad at her. I was just mad. No particular reason. Anyone would have done. Just mad. I turned and walked back to my bus bench.

"Son, I'm going to pray that you're loosed from that bondage," she said.

That didn't even rate a response from me. I turned my back to the old lady and waved her off with my hand.

Shit! Where in the fuck is the bus? My nose is starting to drip, I thought to myself.

While I was sitting there, something the old lady had said kept moving around in my head. It was the phrase *going to hell, going to hell.* It made me remember something I hadn't thought about in years—the first time I OD'd on heroin back in 1975 or 1976.

A friend of mine (another deviant) and I had been shooting dope and drinking all day. Though I had been drinking for years prior, I had just recently started shooting dope intravenously. At the time I owned my own home. I had a wonderful job I loved (airport skycap). I ran a gambling shack on the weekends. I had money to burn. "Look, Ma! I'm on top of the world." By nightfall, I wanted to do another of my new favorites, a speedball, a mixture of heroin and cocaine.

At the time, I would have sworn on a stack of Bibles that this and this alone was the Holy Grail of drug sensation, the shortcut to peace on earth and goodwill toward men, the secret ingredient of bliss and contentment—in short, Nirvana.

We could hardly contain our anticipation as we licked our lips and our smirks broadened. Facsimiles of life invaded our eyes with light as the King, heroin, and the Queen, cocaine, were mixed together in the cooker, drawn up through the cotton into the syringe, and then, through the needle, enticed into the vein.

Nothing, but nothing could withstand the power of the speedball, the feeling of euphoria as it replaces every sensation in the body from the tip of your head to the bottom of your feet—instantly—as you push the golden-colored elixir into your being. You know you can't feel any better; it's just not possible.

Then you slowly, slowly start to pull the plunger back up the syringe. As the syringe slowly starts to fill with blood, your nose starts to fill with the cool aroma of cocaine from the inside out.

Simultaneously, the mouth is invaded with the taste and freeze of cocaine on each taste bud. The exhilaration of the speed permeates every cell of the body at the same time. The rush to your private place is instantaneous.

Pushing the plunger back down reasserts the King's influence over your body, and the euphoric cycle begins again. In-out, in-out—it feels so good you never want to stop jacking the plunger off. In-out, up-down, in-out, speeding, nodding, up-down, speeding, nodding. I can see it now in my mind's eye, what it was like and how it used to feel.

It's like always living in the dark and cold and then seeing the sun and feeling its warmth for the first time. You'll never forget it. You can always see it and feel it in your mind's eye.

The speedball feels so good to an addict that you don't want to stop jacking the outfit (syringe) off. If you don't stop and continue to jack off, you can short-circuit your heart by the extreme speed-and-downer action. It feels so good to an addict that many will short circuit their heart instead of stopping.

That's what I was thinking as I sat waiting for the bus, after the intrusion of the old-lady Bible-thumper.

I remembered sitting in my back bedroom with my partner, neither one of us talking much, just sitting there jacking off the outfit, in and out, in and out, in and out, so good, so good. All of a sudden—I don't know how—but all of a sudden I was watching this movie.

I didn't see the outline of a screen or the borders of a TV. The movie was going kind of fast, like when you hit the rewind button on a VCR, except with a tape you rewind from the end to the beginning. At first, I didn't realize what movie I was watching, but toward the end I realized I was the star of the movie. It was me! It was about me, but unlike a tape, this movie was rewinding from beginning to the end. By the time I figured out what I was watching was my life being rerun right in front of me, I was at the end. I had no idea how long this took. By the time it registered, I was watching myself sitting in the back bedroom. Just as suddenly as I had started watching the movie of me, I was in a black place that seemed to be a tunnel, and I was flying. I don't mean flying like Superman. I was standing straight up and down, and I was moving and the sensation of movement was very fast.

Off in the distance, I could see a bright light, and I was coming up on it very fast. That's when the thought came to me: *I must be dead.* I had no anxiety about the thought, *I must be dead.* It seemed somewhat natural, a matter of fact, but I was extremely curious about what I looked like if I was dead.

I remember looking down at myself. The first thing I noticed was my feet. They were pointy at the ends. They were also very black. I looked at myself, and I looked just like a shadow. I was a black shadow, flying straight up towards the brightest light I could ever imagine. As bright as this light was, and although I was approaching it quickly, I noticed I wasn't squinting. Seems like I should've been, but I wasn't. Right before I got to the source of this light, I didn't see anything or anyone. I heard something, and to this day I don't know if it was audible or in my mind, but someone said, "Not yet. Not your time."

Like I said, I saw no one, but as soon as I heard that command, I was back in my bedroom on the floor with my friend bending over me, slapping me in the face. He was calling my name over and over—"Ed, Ed, come on man, don't die on me, Ed, Ed." I tried to move, but I couldn't.

My body wouldn't respond to the commands I was giving it. It was as if I wasn't connected, as if I wasn't hooked back up yet. In my mind, I was telling myself to move, but the signal wasn't getting through. I tried to tell my friend, Major, to slap me harder, but only a whisper would come out. He had to put his ear over my mouth. I don't know why, but I felt if he slapped me harder, sensation would return to my body and I would be able to move. It worked, and after about a minute or so of him slapping me hard, I was able to motion with my hand for him to stop. It was only after about an hour that I could fully move about on my own, albeit very weakly.

After that experience, I swore off all alcohol and drugs. I read everything at the time I could about life after death, books by Dr. E. Kubler-Ross, Dr. James Moody, and others. Most of the books I read spoke about the black tunnel with the bright light at the end. They talked about people going through the light and seeing Jesus, about being overwhelmed with this feeling of love, contentment, and serenity. Some people spoke about seeing all their departed friends and loved ones.

The people in the books talked about being in a place beautiful beyond description. Some people claimed they saw angels flying around singing praises to Christ with voices so wonderful they knew they had to be angels.

Well, I don't know about that.

All I know is that I was in what seemed like a black tunnel that had a bright light as I neared the end of it. That's all I saw, and I heard only five words. "Not yet. Not your time."

In all the books I read on near-death or after-death experiences, I found one and only one that said the tunnel I was in was a tunnel to the center of the earth. That the light I saw was the glow from a lake of white-hot lava. That when you passed through the tunnel, two demons on either side of the tunnel entrance would grab your arms with an unbreakable grasp. You would then be taken to a place and tormented until Judgment Day.

Why, with all the books that I read on the subject about people going to a wonderful place and seeing and doing only wonderful things, did I feel in my gut that the tunnel going to the center of the earth was the tunnel I was in? Could it have been my lifestyle, the way I was living?

Well, no matter, my oath of abstinence lasted only about two weeks, if that long, after my death experience. I started drinking and using again. That was over twenty years ago, and I didn't stop using until July 1994.

On the bus bench, the old lady's words, "going to hell," had triggered the memory of that past experience. If I had any doubt about which tunnel I was in then, I had no doubt where I would go if I died today.

In the twenty years since that overdose in my back bedroom, I had progressed from a slickster to a low-down conniving, lying, thieving, steal from his mama, corrupter of innocence, third-degree black belt alcoholic-addict—in intensity and in my dedication to my addiction. If I died today, and there was any kind of cosmic justice, there was no way, no way, I was going to go to a wonderful place where everyone was flying around smiling and singing, "Glory, Glory Hallelujah."

I now know firsthand that when you die, you (or what makes you "you") goes somewhere. Sitting on that bus bench twenty years later, waiting to go buy some dope, it dawned on me. I mean the light bulb went on. If Hell is a real place, if I died right now, I *was going to Hell*. I knew without a doubt, just as sure as I was sitting on a bus bench, heading to buy some dope, that I was going to Hell.

Right at that moment, a feeling of despair and hopelessness came over me so powerfully that I started to weep uncontrollably at the bus stop.

Damn! I don't want to cry, I thought. I tried to stop and couldn't. Shit! I hadn't had any dope yet. People were looking at me. Damn! I didn't cry at my son's funeral. I was too hard an addict to be crying, but I knew I was going to Hell. I didn't want to go; that's why I was crying.

The people around me at the bus stop saw me just start crying and figured I must be shermed up (on PCP), so they started moving away from me. I got up and started walking away from the bus stop, crying all the while.

My heart found these words: *God please, Lord Jesus, I don't want to go to Hell. I don't want to go, but I know I am. I've been hooked too long. I can't stop using. Jesus, I can't and won't stop. Please, Lord, I can't do it by myself. You're the only chance I have. Please have mercy. Save me, please. I don't want to go to Hell.*

Right about then, my bus hit the corner.

I dried my eyes. I was in control again. I didn't know what had come over me. Time was a-wasting. Time for my morning wake-up. *Ha! Ha!* My dope was at hand. I started singing to myself, *The sun is shining. There's plenty of light. A new day is dawning sunny and bright.*

I was the first one on the bus. It wouldn't be long now. Soon I'd have a syringe full of heroin in my arm. What had I been thinking at the bus stop? That old lady must have done something to me. How could I ever think for—a minute that I wanted to withhold my allegiance to the King?

Two days later, unforeseen circumstances put me in a twelve-step program at the Wayback Inn. The Lord had heard my plea.

4

Making Changes

My first thirty days were very hard.

The first two weeks were almost unbearable.

My withdrawal from heroin was brutal. The facility I was in had a "Tough Old School" policy. No drugs were given to help wean me off drugs. I had to go cold turkey.

The first twenty-four hours without any dope in my system, I guess my body thought I was playing; that it was taking me just a little longer to scam up some money to get some medicine, believing the dope was coming any minute. After twenty-four hours, my body started making its demands known.

In the course of a day, subtle sweating and clamminess escalated to sticky, drenching sweat that smelled of stale alcohol and toxic drug waste. Minor nervous stomach developed into knife-stabbing, razor-cutting cramping; vomiting, and dry heaving—par for the course. Flu-like symptoms were steadily increasing in intensity—fever one minute turning into freezing chills the next. No nose action; it was full of mucus. You can only breathe through your mouth, which keeps your mouth and throat raspy dry.

By the second day, all you can do is lie there drenched and smelling from your own funk; you have no energy of your own to move. Your energy came from a daily infusion of dope and alcohol. Your own energy centers ceased to function on their own long ago. Drugs have become your will, your motivation, and your inspiration. Without them for forty-eight hours, you find all you can do is curl up in a ball, sweat, smell, hurt, and wish you were dead.

By the fourth day, every nerve in your body feels like it's on fire. Every movement brings on a grimace from the pain. Every cell in your body is now totally out of its portion of dope and on the warpath, warring against themselves. Mass confusion inside the cell walls without the secret calming balm only drugs can supply.

My misery is increased.

My body wants its medicine, and it wants it now.

Acute diarrhea was added to my assortment of ailments. Most times, I didn't have the energy to get out of the bed in time to make it to the bathroom before wet number two was running down my leg. Here I was, a grown man, shitting on myself two and three times a day.

Even though a man can say he understands the pain and suffering a woman goes through during childbirth, women know all a man can do is imagine what the pain and suffering of childbirth is like. They can never know.

The same is true for a chronic drug abuser going through withdrawal. The pain and suffering can be described, even imagined, but never really understood. Like childbirth, withdrawal can only be experienced by the sufferer. One of the worst aspects of my withdrawal was the sleeplessness. My body said no medicine, no sleep. For five days, I got not one wink of sleep. On the sixth night, my body allowed me to sleep for one hour. Finally, the worst of my withdrawal ordeal was over.

Even now, after ten years without a drug or a drink, I'm still experiencing withdrawal symptoms on a day-to-day basis. Running, stuffy nose, watery eyes, incessant yawning, and muscle spasms still occur. Back then, some counselors I spoke to said since I was a chronic user for so long, it might take a few years for the symptoms to go away altogether. A doctor I spoke to stated, "The symptoms might never go away," a very small price to pay, as far as I'm concerned, for a clean and sober life. Besides, it'll keep me from forgetting where I came from.

One of the things I learned in the program was that I had known about God most of my life, just as I had known about drugs and alcohol most of my life. The difference was that I had a working relationship with drugs and alcohol, not with God. They said I had to know and believe in a power greater than myself, surrender my will and my life to this power and, like steps three and eleven in Alcoholics Anonymous suggest, understand this power, and that's all. What an order! How can a mortal man understand an immortal God? How do we understand anything?

Understanding means comprehension, tolerance, mutual agreement. I'd have to learn about my Higher Power and try to understand Him. I was told early on in the program that I could use a light bulb for my Higher Power, but after I read the instructions on the side of the box, I saw there wasn't much more knowledge to gain from it. I was told I could use a chair, a doorknob, or the universe as a Higher Power. Accepting a doorknob as my Higher Power somehow just didn't work for me. I comprehended a chair pretty good, but I felt a chair didn't have much to offer to help me with my problem. I didn't know what type of mutual agreement I could work out with the universe.

I remembered the God that I had always known. The God I believed was out there somewhere. I just didn't know what He was about. Besides, this Higher Power had left sixty-six books about Himself. I decided to gain knowledge about Him to see if He could accept my will and life. To find out how tolerant He was of people who made mistakes. To see if we could come to a mutual agreement—Him taking my addiction for my seeking His will.

There are some in the twelve-step programs who say I shouldn't mention the name of the Higher Power that worked and continues to work in my life. But this story is about me and the Higher Power that turned me from my path of destruction. That Higher Power was and is Jesus Christ, the Son of the living God.

I was told that this was a program about change.

I had to change everything about me. I began to see what had always been the problem in the past whenever I had tried to stop drinking and using. I would abstain from drugs and alcohol for a short period, but I would continue to be in the same places, do the same things, hang with the same people, and have the same perceptions and reactions to external stimuli, a.k.a., life.

Nothing had really changed.

I was still the same leopard with the same spots. It was just a matter of time (and usually a short time) before I used and drank again. I had to change not outwardly but from within, from the inside out. My perceptions and reactions had to change, but how? By reading and learning more about my Higher Power, believing and praying for His will and not mine, asking for His words and putting my small belief into action. I believe I was given this:

Making Changes

If you want to change your behavior
Make Jesus Christ your Lord and Savior
He will turn your life around
Pick you up when you're on the ground
Just trust in Him and do not falter
Jesus will be your Rock of Gibraltar
If you're going down with drugs or drink
Remember, on the water Jesus didn't let Peter sink
Jesus is our only lifeline

He shed His blood; He paid the fine
Alcohol and drugs are spirits, true
But Christ can ban them out of you
Do step one and submit to the Master
And watch your Recovery be that much faster

I wanted to change my behavior. The Lord showed me the way through Him. He could do what I could not do myself, just trust Him. He had already paid for my deliverance. *Jesus* is my Rock. He is steadfast. He will not change. And He is there for me.

5

A Way Out

The twelve-step program I was in taught that alcoholics and addicts have a disease, a disease of a three-fold nature, a spiritual malady that affects mind and body. Our body becomes diseased, our mind corrupted, and our spirit bankrupt. We get what I call "reversal syndrome." We start thinking backwards, a complete turnaround in our thinking. The more we come to depend on drugs and alcohol, the more we come to believe that what's good for us is bad and what's bad for us is good.

Relationships with family and close friends are destroyed because of our behavior. We eventually lose our jobs or stagnate in them because we have become unproductive and ineffective. We forget our goals, if we ever had any, and opportunities are never realized. Your self-esteem and confidence come only out of a bottle, through a pipe, or by a syringe firmly planted in a vein. Instead of embracing life and all it has to offer, we rush headlong into destructive oblivion. We move faster and faster toward the goal line of utter despair and hopelessness, defeated seemingly by our own hands.

At the base of our addiction lies our spiritual malady, our spiritual bankruptcy, for we have nothing in our spiritual accounts. The success of our recovery relies on *change,* from inside out. We need a spiritual awakening as to why we're in the spiritual shape we're in.

Nothing said it better than Ephesians 6:11–12:

> Put on the whole armor of God that ye may be able to stand against the wiles of the devil. For we wrestle not against flesh and blood; but against principalities, against powers, against the rulers of the darkness of this world, against *spiritual* wickedness in high places. [italics mine]

Once you realize that you are spiritually bankrupt, you need to find a way out of that condition. There is what seems to be reversal on the spiritual plane, because for you to win in the spiritual realm, you must surrender on this physical plane. That's right—surrender to win. You must admit that you are powerless over your spiritual malady and turn your will and your life over to a *Higher Power*, a power that can restore your spiritual stability and your mental sanity. These were my first steps toward a way out:

A Way Out

Lord, please bless me to overcome
From myself I can no longer run
At first the drugs would let me escape
Shield me from my doubt and self-hate
At first peer pressure, then for pleasure
Alcohol and Drugs became my treasure
More valued than money, for I'd sell all I had
For a drink or a rock or another dime bag
Saw most of my friends go from cars to pushing baskets
Knew a few more that went from baskets to filling caskets
Make women and girls walk the streets late at night
Trying to sell what they got with all of their might
Risking their life with each car they get in
Seeking and Freaking, some never seen again
This disease is not partial, because quite a few men
Will get down on their knees, or their backs they will bend
Many are blind to the fact and don't know that they're sick
They think that they like it, are weak, or just need a fix
The disease is cunning, baffling, and takes its toll hour by hour
The start of a cure is to admit that we're powerless and seek the
    Higher Power
AA, NA, CA, too—they all have the steps; they'll show you what to
    do
Trust your Higher Power; believe He's there for you
Not only will you not use; you'll have a Spiritual Awakening too

Slowly, I began to realize that I couldn't make a change from within. I had to be open and willing to have a Higher Power, one of my understanding, change me.

6

Finding Out

My control over my destiny had brought me to where I was today; sitting here in the Wayback Inn, a dope fiend for over twenty years. I wanted to change but how? I had to give up the reins of my life to another more qualified than me (St. John 1: 26–27). I had to trust. I had to believe. For once, I had to be still and let it happen. I was staying in a live-in program while I was learning to be still. We (addicts in the program) were confined to a single dwelling structure with limited access to the outside world. This left plenty of time for past reflections. This is one of the things I found out about myself:

Finding Out

Before my very first drink, I didn't have a clue
That with a little booze, with your ass I could tell you what to do
With a few drinks under my belt, it was easy to tell you what you
 needed to know
And if you didn't like it, you could kiss my ass then go

With alcohol by my side, we were a team that couldn't be beat
Under the influence of that mighty spirit, I knew we could
 accomplish any feat
With alcohol coursing through my veins I'd heed no limitations; my
 desires held no bounds
I held liquid magic in a bottle and thanked the God Bacchus for the
 boldness-making elixir I had found

At first I didn't notice, for more meant better, so more of my magic potion I would take

For it took more and more to quiet that increasing whisper in my head that kept saying *fake, fake, fake*

(I'd start drinking in the morning, 'cause that voice would start to whisper as soon as I'd awake)

I would drink doubles all through lunch time, and start feeling the rest of the day was going to be a piece of cake

By quitting time, the voice was still, but my head was saying *get more* and a beeline to the bar I'd make

Less and less of my drinking escapades I'd remember, for blackouts had become part of my norm

The whisper was now a shout, and the idea I couldn't stop had begun to form

People started being jealous of me and would work against me whenever they could

Envious because I was the life of the party or because I didn't have to do what I should

They'd complain because I would be late a few times a week at the job and sometimes not show up at all

Or when I'd give 'em what for down at the pub, some would act appalled

Drinking would make me clumsy sometimes, but it was a small price to pay

For being that one, that son of a gun, who knew how to work but more importantly how to play

Soon drinking became the answer for whatever emotion I'd feel

I discovered I'd escape that much quicker if along with my drink I'd take a pill

What was I running from? Just reality and myself

After years of trying with drugs and alcohol I realized I couldn't do it and needed help

I sought help but couldn't admit I was powerless, so I was doomed to another run

Other people could control their drinking; why couldn't my drinking be like theirs, just fun?

I had to lose everything to drinking—family, job, and friends

Self-esteem, self-respect; I was only left with what I'd tried to run from in the end

Left with myself, and reality, all I could do was break down and cry

Forced to look back on the wreckage of my past and what my life had become; between sobs all I could say was why?

Why me, God? Why was I singled out? I cried because of the self-pity I felt

Then, in a moment of clarity, I asked God for His help

I admitted I couldn't do it alone. I was powerless and without His help I was through

Take my life and my will and do with it whatever you will do

The God of my understanding put people in my life who showed me the way

Showed me how to stop drinking and using, not forever but day by day

Introduced me to twelve steps that, when practiced, would show me what it is to truly live

How to be grateful, have compassion, and with others be willing to give

Realize there's a Power greater than me, and spiritual with Him I should be

Practice these twelve steps and from the bondage of alcohol and drugs. He will set you free

7

Feelings

Everyone is different.

But I truly believe a live-in program, an extended live-in program, was necessary in any attempt to turn my life around. I needed a safe environment where I was shielded from the access to and influence of drugs and alcohol, a safe environment where I was constantly bombarded with positive reinforcement and information about the whys of addiction (and the who's, as in, who's really doing these things to me?). I needed to be somewhere where I could learn who and what I really was, beyond my mental image of who I was, a place I could learn about quitting, denial, facing up, about twelve steps, surrender, and understanding my Higher Power.

This live-in program was my incubation period, my gestation for a new life. During this time, the counselors constantly encouraged us to get in touch with our feelings—not only what we felt but why we felt that way. There were "group feelings" sessions about "How did you feel when you did this?" or "Why did you feel that when that person did that?" And always, "How are you feeling today?" One day, after automatically telling a counselor, "I feel okay," I thought to myself, *You're here to change, so you have to put forth some effort. So what are you really feeling about what you feel?* After some thought, I realized this was what I felt about my feelings:

Feelings

I see my feelings as an ocean
Vast, immense, deep, very deep, some depths unfathomable, except
 to *God*
Potentially life giving, or life taking—take your pick, either or

My feelings, like the ocean, are in a state of being
Constantly constant and forever changing
The waves of my emotions beat against the shores of my
    consciousness

Sometimes a gentle lapping on the beach of my awareness
Other times, breakers pounding the surf of my existence
Who can control the ocean?

When winds of destiny continuously move across it
From North, South, East and West
Gentle breezes of joy or frustration?

Strong winds of anxiety or despair
Gale-force anger or passion
Who can still my ocean?

Who can calm my winds?
Clouds of insecurity span the horizon of my newly found sobriety
Will the tempest of emotions again dash the hope of freedom from
    addiction against the rocks of defeat?

Once more, must I drown in an ocean of uncertainty?
Buffeted by winds of fear, loneliness, doubt, and self-hate coming to
    rest in the depths of addiction?
Who can still my ocean?
Who can calm my winds?

There is *one*
Whose hand can calm the waters
Whose words can still the winds

Not me—but a Power greater than me
The *God* of my own understanding
There's a *God* for you in the twelve steps
Who can calm your waters and still your winds
May you find Him now

Yes, feelings change—like the weather, like the wind, and like the ocean. Early in my disease of addiction, feelings had been excellent triggers for me to drink and get high. *I don't feel good, I'm tried, You can't talk to me that way,* or *She doesn't treat me with the respect that I deserve. I'm happy, I'm sad, I'm hungry, I'm full, I'm horny, so why don't I get a little hit or a drink first.*

Later in my disease/addiction, I told myself I had no feelings. I no longer needed them. I cared for nothing and no one. I needed no excuse to get high; drinking and doping was all there was. What was there to feel about? Just get the booze and the dope. Just do it. Fuck feelings. Straight denial—that's what I was in, denial.

8

Imaginary Line

Alcoholics and addicts surround themselves within a veil of denial. Many never become aware that they are looking at the world through it. You see, I really did have feelings. In fact, I was in pain, extreme pain, as I acknowledge later. I had a disease of a three-fold nature—physical, mental, and spiritual. With each drink from the short dog (wine), each puff on the pipe (cocaine) and the sherm (PCP), each shot (heroin) into the arm, I was murdering; I was killing my inner man. My spirit was crying out for help, begging me to stop, but I wouldn't hear. I couldn't hear. I felt nothing from my spirit, for I kept myself numb with alcohol and drugs. My spirit's slow death affected my mental stability, which in turn affected my physical well-being. It was easier to continue on the path of destruction I was on than to part the veil of denial through which I was looking at the world.

I was numbing myself daily so I wouldn't feel the pain or the stirring from within, effectively putting a muzzle on my conscience. I wore denial around me so completely that not one iota of reality got through. When reality did get through and invade my senses, I would scramble to get a drink, hit, or fix. It was too painful to acknowledge what I had become, what I was doing, and to whom and with whom I was doing it. Too painful to concede how readily and passively I accepted larger and larger doses of negativity. Too painful to see how far I had strayed from what I had been taught, from what I *knew* was right. Too painful to stop and see how many people I had affected with hate, rage, and despair. Too painful to count how many bridges I had burned. Too painful to acknowledge the ruined relationships in my wake. And too painful to give an account of what I had done. No, denial was an easier place to live, or so I thought. Eventually, even the rent there became too high to pay.

For decades I was in denial.

I closed my eyes to what was really going on in my life. Closed my eyes to what I had become and what my real final destination would be: jails, institutions, or death. *Man, when did this start? I've been getting loaded so long, it seems like I've been getting high forever since day one.* But it had to have started somewhere. When did it become too late. When did I cross over? As I pondered that, I was given this:

Imaginary Line

Sometimes I try to remember when I took that fateful step

Try to remember if I felt the transition from living hope to the place where fear is kept

Yes, fear, despair, and loneliness kept there; also hate, rage, and death you'll find

All waiting to embrace you when you cross that imaginary line

Where was the crossover from normal to obsessed?

When did I stop being that good friend and become that neighborhood pest?

When did Mr. Punctual stop caring about the time?

What drink or drug was I using when I crossed that imaginary line?

When did a drink stop being a drink; when did a drink become a drunk?

When did the caring about good morals become not caring how low I had sunk?

How did the role model who stood for something become the man without a spine?

The man who would soon stand for nothing when he crossed that imaginary line

When did social use become a game that's played for keeps?

How many steps did it take from being a man of means to a man living on the streets?

Where was the transformation from a connoisseur of fine spirits to a seeker of $2.00 wine?

When was it too late? Can I ever step back over that imaginary line?

Most lines in life are boundaries—you know how far you can go
But this disease so blinds you, you never see, you never know
Where did your life as a normie end and the birth of the addict
    intertwine?
At what point did I cross that imaginary line?

Once you cross the line, you never can step back
You'll always be an alcoholic or an addict; believe me—that's a fact
There is One who can help you; just surrender and in time
Though you can't step back, you'll no longer have to use or drink on
    that side of the imaginary line

He's a *God* of your own understanding, a restorer of sanity
Still an alcoholic or an addict, but recovered you can be
Turn your will and your life over to your *higher one* and He will set
    you free
His love and understanding will heal you when you cross the line,
    imaginary

I crossed the imaginary line back in the 1970s and didn't even realize I had
made the transition from social to obsessed until many years later. Some of you
reading this have crossed that imaginary line too. Some of you haven't crossed it
yet. Check yourself. Where are you in relationship to your line. Are you getting
ready to cross it, or have you already crossed? Check yourself. You have nothing
to lose but time, time you'll never get back.

9

Ninety-Day Wonder

A live-in program is a wonderful opportunity, but only if you're ready for change, real change, in your concept of what it means to live.

A live-in program gives you firsthand insight into how other people did it, how they changed their lives for the better. You get this insight at the AA, NA, and CA meetings you're required to attend while you're there. At the meetings, people with varying lengths of sobriety tell you what it was like while they were getting loaded, how they got sober, and what they're doing to stay sober. While I was there, one theme came up over and over in their stories: relapse.

Many of them were on the road of sobriety, when seemingly all of a sudden—blam!—they were drinking or using again. Some had been sober for years when this happened. For most, relapse occurred early in their sobriety. I really listened to what they had to say about why they felt they had slipped. I not only listened to their stories, but I heeded their suggestions for avoiding those pitfalls. I was fairly new in my new walk towards sobriety.

I was feeling pretty good, and was told I was looking pretty good. The thought actually entered my head that I had been in the program long enough, that I was fine now. I didn't need no sponsor telling me what to do. I, me, could take care of myself. I thank the *Lord* that *He* gave me these thoughts before I could act on the "I'm okay" thoughts:

Ninety-Day Wonder

Thirty-, sixty-, ninety-day chip. I'm feeling pretty good now, and I know I won't slip

My skin's looking good, I've gained some weight, and the recovery thing? I've got it whipped

I've read the Big Book, well at least up to page 164

I've read the twelve steps over and over until reading them became
more like a chore

I can't wait to get back around my old buddies and show them I'm
cured

Show them my ninety-day chip, because with that I know my
sobriety is assured

That they're still drinking and using won't bother me in the least

I've fought back the disease for ninety days; I can let my mind rest in
peace

A lot of those old timers said you had to get with *God*, and Spiritually
you must become awake

Man, I'm not into that old *God* thing, and that old Spiritual stuff was
more than I could take

I worked the program my way, because I know what's best for me

I don't need to keep going to no meetings; I'll stay clean and
sober—just wait and see

Sponsor? Sponsor who? I don't need nobody telling me what I can
and cannot do

A sponsor can't know what's happening in the real world. I bet they
don't have a clue

I'm free from drinking, I'm cured, I'm ninety days clean

I'll never drink and use again, and to you I don't care how it seems

Yes, I was a ninety-day wonder, and I knew that I knew that I knew

You couldn't make me believe that in ninety-five days, my sobriety
would be through

That was over a year ago, a year plus ninety days, by the way

And looking back with hindsight, I'm glad it happened, I might say

You see, I didn't do anything but abstain from drinking for a period
of ninety days

I had not one day of recovery, because I had to do it my way

I didn't admit I was powerless; I didn't believe in a Power greater
than me

I couldn't turn my life and my will over to a *God* as I understood
Him, because I just couldn't see

Now I know only *God* can give sobriety, and it's a little part I play

Just trying to work twelve steps in my life, and just trying to work it
day by day

Being humble is what I learned, and believe me, I'm not trying to
steal your thunder

But this is a lesson you will learn if you feel you're going to be a
ninety-day wonder

In the program, we learn that most alcoholics and addicts are insane. By that I mean we constantly do the same things and expect different results. We try to recover in sobriety, but we go back to the same places we got high in, associate with the same people, and do the same things, yet expect different results.

Insanity.

This was my second program, a six-month program. My first program had been a ninety-day program. I left that program after ninety days, and within five days I was drinking and using dope again. Why had I thought I could leave this second program after ninety days and be all right.

Insanity.

The disease is cunning, baffling, and powerful. I already knew ninety days was not enough for me. I had tried it before with disastrous results, but here I was, ready to do the same thing again, expecting different results.

Crazy.

This time had to be different. I had to wait for the miracle. I had to be willing for it to happen. I had to believe a Power greater than me could make it happen. I had to surrender. I had to give up any illusion that I could be the captain of my own ship. How many times had my life run aground with me at the helm?

Insanity, doing the same thing and expecting different results.

10

Winner

I had always thought of myself as a winner. I mean, I had always been capable. I almost always got my way, and I virtually always ran the show. Being in the program gave me time to stop and really look at what type of winner I was:

The Winner

The cry of victory, the shouts from the crowd
As I made it toward the goal post, the stadium went wild
Yes, another touchdown, the crowd cheering on its feet
Always a winner, never a loser, always in my mind but not out here
    on the streets

I stole the pass and twirled around
The crowd could sense what was going down
I dribbled left, I dribbled right
I ran for the basket with all my might

I jump and shoot and then the cheering
Go, Go, Go from the crowd was all I was hearing
I'm so good, how much more can this crowd take?
Then I'm back out on the street, feeling no higher than a snake

Always in the limelight, forever the victor within my head
In reality, the cycle of alcohol and drugs makes you wish that you
    were dead

Daydreams become so attractive when your nightmares become so
   real
Numbing yourself with drug and drink, so you don't think or feel

When drinking and using becomes your most conscious thought
It's easy for the rest of you to dream of what you're not
This demoralizing behavior can only end one way
Jails, Institutions, and Death will become the order of your day

You fall under the delusion that your real life is an illusion
You're okay, your life's all right, just taper off is your conclusion
But you know the taper-off part is just a lie
More delusion, more daydreaming, more pie in the sky

You reach a point in a moment of clarity and say, I just gotta stop
   using
At the same moment, you realize your whole existence has become
   abusing
You cannot stop, you cannot go on
Hopelessness, Powerlessness, using again—it's the same old song

Not wanting to keep on living, to cowardly to outright die
Self-esteem rating is zero, self-hate rating very high
Fear, Disgust, and Loneliness were all waiting in the wings
To take the place of the daydreams that once brought solace; but no
   longer comfort could they bring

Oooh! The vicious cycle repeating the same old thing
Am I doomed forever to using and abusing, is misery the only song
   that my life can sing?
Why can't I get it, why am I different from everyone else?
My head said I can do it, I'm a winner, like always, just rely on self

Finally, my life has become unmanageable, everything just falling
   apart
Again I found myself calling out *God, God,* somebody help me please,
   but this time it was from the heart

I was led to an anonymous organization that spoke of a Higher
Power, greater than me
They said just to surrender, and that would be my only fee

Since then I've come to believe in a *God* of my own understanding,
and I've turned my will and my life over to Him
He's restoring me to sanity. He's my *God* and plus He's my friend
There might be other ways, but for me there is only one
A twelve-step program, a *God* of my own understanding, with Power
through *His Son*

Yeah, some winner I turned out to be. I never won at what I now deem as important—a relationship with a woman, my family, or my children. I never won at self-esteem. I always had to prove myself to keep up with the image I thought others had of me. I never won at believing there was a *God* out there that really cared about me. I was alone. It was up to me to sink or swim. I had to win; that's what life was all about. To the victor went the spoils. I had to win, even though I had been steadily losing ground for the past thirty years.

11

Surrender to Win

There's a slogan floating around in the program that says, "You have to surrender to win." Hell! Surrender to win? That's contrary to just about everything the world system teaches us about success. But this is supposed to be a spiritual program. Spiritual goals are contrary to worldly values. Surrender to win. Even if I thought it might work, how do you surrender? On top of that, how do you surrender to something you can't even see? While I pondered that, I was given this:

Surrender to Win

A rose by any other name would smell just as sweet
A drunk is still a drunk whether he's in a suit or living on the streets
A crack head is a smoker whether he's smoking in the boardroom or
    behind a green trash bin
A junkie is a state of mind; whether lowdown or highbrow makes no
    difference when the needle's pushed in

The disease of alcoholism and addiction is progressive, whether
    you're a beginner or an old pro
And if your body is afflicted with the allergy that starts the craving,
    your obsession can only grow
Followed by the denial that most will practice for years on end
Knowing deep down within that we're hooked, are alcoholics, are
    hopeless and most likely this is the way our life we'll spend

Some can learn to change with not much damage, but most of us go
    to the curb
Jails, institutions, and death is our lot in life, because many refuse to
    hear the word

That word is AA, NA, CA, or that there's a way you can stop, really
   stop, and start to live

There's a Power out there that's greater than you, and to this power
   your addiction you can give

You must admit you're powerless, that you've done everything that
   you knew to do

But that still isn't enough, you have to give up, turn your life and will
   over to the Power that can do it for you

Just be willing and tired of things going the same old way

Believe you can be restored to sanity; it will happen day by day

For more than twenty years I tried to do it my way and paid with
   endless misery and despair

I'd given up early on, I just existed, if it wasn't alcohol or drugs I
   didn't care

Hopeless, angry, self-hating, and bitter, I knew I was doomed and
   just waited for the end

I was tired of being tired, and then I heard if I was ready to surrender,
   I could win

Surrender to win meant to admit I was powerless and that I had to
   turn my will and my life over to another

Not father, mother, brother, sister, or friend, only to a Power greater,
   a *God* of my understanding, and no other

By the power of my own will, my life had come to mean the same
   thing as fail

My only hope and chance was to surrender to a Power greater, if my
   life was to prevail

If sobriety is your goal, certain things you must do; if misery you
   don't want to repeat

Recovery without surrender is a near impossible feat

Surrender to your *Higher Power* and win, for that Power has never
   lost

Serenity, peace, sobriety will become the new values of your life, pain
   and misery never again being the cost

I had to surrender. I wanted to win at life. There's another cliché in live-in programs that says, "Don't leave before the miracle happens." I really wanted this time to be different. I truly didn't want to drink or use again. However, I didn't know how I could make it happen. I believed a power greater than me could remake me for the better. I was willing to give Him control of my life. I believed He could, and I was willing to wait for the miracle to happen. Even though I had been in the program ninety days and was feeling pretty good about myself, I decided to stay and not leave the program. I would wait on the miracle.

12

Puff-Puff

As I thought about the miracle, I just happened to glance over at a friend who was in the program. First, let me say that the live-in program I was in was a co-ed program, meaning there were men and women housed under the same roof. This friend I mentioned was a woman that came into the program a month after I did. Looking at her now as compared to then, I could see some visual transformation or miracle had taken place on her.

Her skin shone with a healthy glow. Her hair looked like strands of silk. She had a face I could look at all day long and never get tired of and a body that was obedient to teenage proportions. Man, I knew in my heart if I just had her by my side, everything would be all right. That's what I thought about her now. Sixty days earlier, when I first saw her, that's not what I thought. You see, she had come in with a severe rock cocaine addiction.

Women in the beginning stages of addiction are called "strawberries" on the streets. A strawberry is a woman who'll trade sex for a hit on the pipe. (Men who'll do the same thing are called "raspberries.") As the addiction becomes more severe eating food, and sleep are replaced by constant smoking of the rock, eventually the woman becomes a "curb creature." That means she lives at the curb, next to the gutter, trying to barter sex, oral and otherwise, for a hit of the rock. She becomes a smoker, a puffer of the first order. Everything she has she'll trade for a puff on the pipe.

A curb creature has progressed from selling her body to begging people to use her body for a puff on the pipe. When my friend first came through the doors of the WayBack Inn, she was a 95-pound puffer who looked like she had never heard the sound of running water or smelled the fragrance of soap. She was to the curb. As I thought about the first time I saw her, later that night, I was given these words about *puffers*:

Puff-Puff

Puff-Puff here
Puff-Puff there
Puffing in the day time, Puffin' through the night
Puffing becomes a career, no other goals in sight

Peeking out the windows, everyone's a cop
Everybody's watching you; they know you hit the Rock
Puffing with Barcardi, 151's the lick
Winding up with those car antennas and a flick of the Bic

Puffing in the doorways, back against the wind
Puffing in the alleyways, behind those green trash bins
Ducking in that empty house to join the Puffers there
Hoping someone will want to piece up, spend their last bus fare

Playing the pick-up game. Oh yeah! You know the one. Where you
    crawl around on the rugs
Scoring points for picking lint, white pebbles, and dead bugs
Most ladies start out being puffers, but eventually they'll fall
To sucking pricks and turning tricks in somebody's car or behind
    some wall

Let's not leave out the men, who started puffing to be slick
Puffing to get the girls and rock their world, then leave them and call
    them sick
Men who started out being hunters, hunting Strawberries by the
    score
Ending up giving blowjobs or with their own butts up, head to the
    floor

Alcohol has a Spirit, Cocaine and Heroin too
Eventually the Spirit of your drug of choice will totally possess you
    through and through

And the times you choose to use will no longer be up to you
Your Obsession will say *all* the time and there's nothing you can do

Puff-Puff here
Puff-Puff there
If you're a Puffer you know what I say is true
And if you've tried *all else*, I know what will work for you

There's the *steps*, one through twelve, and they'll work just fine
And they're based in the changing of your mind
But you'll need Spiritual help to bring about this change
Allah, Krishna, Buddha, just to name a few
But for me, the Lord Jesus is His name

13

Over-Association

In sixty days' time, she had been changed outwardly from a beast to a beauty. I too was told that I was starting to look human again. Women seemed to be paying more attention to me, especially my friend. I must admit, she seemed to be taking up more and more space in my head. I was thinking about her all the time, and I never missed an opportunity to be near her. I was friendly with all the women in the program, but she was special.

These friendly feelings did not go unnoticed by the staff of counselors at the Wayback Inn. I was informed by the O.A. (over-association) specialist that I was in jeopardy of receiving penalty sanctions if I didn't cease being so friendly with the ladies. In a co-ed program, you can't be seen spending too much time with the same person of the opposite sex.

Talking to or being with the same person too often signals warning bells. The theory is that "transference" may be occurring. Transference happens when an addict switches addictions from one focus to another. The disease of addiction is cunning, baffling, and powerful. The force behind addiction doesn't care what you're hooked on (TV, gossip, cigarettes, soda, food, candy, sex), just as long as you're hooked. When people in the program start to dry out, start getting three square meals a day, and start to fill out a little, the face and hair start to take on a healthy glow. Lingering glances start coming from the opposite sex, and appreciative smiles become more apparent.

Cunning, baffling, the disease starts to ease denial back into the thought process. You start to think, *I don't really have a drug problem; I just needed to cool out for a minute. That girl really likes me; I can tell by the way she looks at me. If I had that person's love, we could make it, just rely on each other. I'm not really an alcoholic or an addict; I just need to be loved by someone, really loved, that's all. I know I, me, self, can do it—together we can do it. I know it'll be different this time.*

Insanity.

The O.A. specialist at the Wayback stayed on me. Couldn't he understand that women just liked to talk to me? Why should he complain if I was popular? He finally instructed the women in the program to stay away from me. I was even banned from sitting next to any women in the dining room area when we ate.

I never admitted it to him (O.A. Specialist), but I was feeling more than friendly toward a couple of the women in the program. If he hadn't harangued me, serious jeopardy may have fallen on my early sobriety. But because of his constant attention, I had to take a serious look at what I was doing and why. My Higher Power gave me this in answer to my prayers about it:

O.A.
(Over-Association)

I didn't see it coming, or if I did I was blind to the fact

I had no defense, I wasn't ready, it was like being broadsided from the back

I didn't know, wasn't even aware I had been bitten by that mythical bug

For all intents and purposes, from the intense emotion that flowed, I knew I had to be in love

I'm already in a relationship with a girl that's good and kind

I live in a recovery house, working a twelve-step program, beginning a relationship with my Higher Power, and everything was fine

New relationships are discouraged in a recovery house; you can lose sight of why you're there, neglect the power from above

And usually it's for all the wrong reasons you find yourself falling in love

We've admitted we were powerless, and over our lives we had no control

Trying to manage a relationship would take the focus off what we were trying to do as making love becomes our goal

We're trying to believe a power greater can restore us to sanity, better than before our alcoholic fall

You're warned that with new love in early sobriety, your recovery will get stalled

All alcoholics and addicts need love, need it more than most

But we must be free from the bondage of addiction before any love we can boast

Must be free to first love self, before we can look to love another

Save our own life, before we risk the life of any other

14

One Day at a Time

Free from the influence of alcohol and drugs for over 120 days, I was beginning to think a little more clearly and rationally. I realized the love and mercy of my Higher Power. He was affording me another chance to save my life, giving me another opportunity to free myself from the bondage of addiction. I could be free if I just allowed Him to free me, for He had the Power to do so.

Not only freedom from addiction.

I took advantage of this time to start healing and recovering from the guilt of failed relationships. The disease of alcoholism and addiction is akin to a deadly virus or a radioactive isotope. The closer someone is to you, the more they are to be contaminated with the disease. The longer you're around an addict, the more he or she becomes over-exposed. Most don't even know why they're ailing until the anger, hurt, and resentment start to manifest physically. As long as I was out there, trying to stay high every minute, I didn't have to think about the hurt, anger, and resentment I was generating in the people closest to me.

With denial coming off layer by layer, I finally got to the point where I had to look at the relationships addiction had shielded me from seeing. I prayerfully asked my Higher Power for help in this area, because I saw no repair myself. I've stated before that I remained in this program for six months. In that time, I think I talked to my daughter twice, maybe three times, on the phone. She chose not to come see me even once during the time I was in the program, even though we were in the same city. This was neither right nor wrong; it just depends which side of the coin you're looking at. I know drugs and alcohol were the root causes of that effect. For decades, the drugs and alcohol affected me negatively. For decades, I affected my family the same way.

What's the biblical saying? "You reap what you sow."

The father-and-child closeness, which can only come with time and growth, was lost to the past. The *God*-given natural closeness between father and child was replaced with an awkward performance that I wished was real.

I'm responsible.

The self-will decisions I made early on definitely affected the course of my life and made waves in the lives of others. I'm responsible, but I can't go back into the past to make it better. Being a recovering alcoholic/addict, I have to accept things the way they are and deal with it. And I will deal with it, for today I deal with situations by praying to my Higher Power, the *God* of my own understanding, who is called *Jesus* the *Christ*. And I do it one day at a time.

One Day at a Time

A new day is here, but it's still just the same
It's just like before, only the name as been changed
Monday, Tuesday, Wednesday, every day of the week
When nothing ever changes, the world seems so bleak

The daily agenda dictates only one thing you must do
Get the drugs and alcohol and whatever else will get you through
What's the difference in a day when you only have one thought
To do the thing that you do best, find somewhere to cop

I've tried to change the record, but it plays on just the same
All my solutions and good intentions by day's end have been in vain
All days have turned to one; is this it, the purpose of my life
Always, forever an addict, doomed to loneliness, fear, and strife?

Hopelessness overwhelmed me, despair constantly in my face
That nagging voice in my head saying, go on, get out of this human
    race
Day in, day out, the voice would shout, go ahead you've got no
    reason to live
The world doesn't need a leech like you, always take, never give

I cried out in my agony *God*, *God*, Help Me Please
I'm powerless, I cannot cope; life's brought me to my knees
I've been to church, but to no avail
They said I was going, but I'm already living in *Hell*

I was introduced to a twelve-step program, and I know it wasn't by
    chance
My Higher Power invited me to this party called life, and man I'm
    going to dance
I'm powerless over alcohol and drugs, but I have found real hope
Day by day, I ask my Higher Power to lead me so I won't stray to or
    act like a dope

My days no longer run together, every day not the same old thing
One day at a time with the peace of mind, willingness to my Higher
    Power will bring
If your days run together, if you think your life is through
Try these steps, seek your Higher Power, and one day your life will
    change for you

15

Poem to My Daughter

No, I can't change my past, but I choose now to let my Higher Power guide my future. I put the relationship with my daughter (Tiffaney) in the hands of my *God* and simply believe He is able to help me. It would be so much easier if I could say, "I just looked around one day and she was grown." But that's not true. The fact is, I missed most of her growing-up time because I was selfish.

A Glimpse of Tiffaney's Cost/View of my Addiction (I–IV)
(In Her Own Words)

I. The Drive-In (Age 8)

Tonight my dad took us to the movies. I was excited, because I loved riding in the back of his van getting thrown all around. Plus, I got to hide under the big beanbag pillow he kept back there. Once we arrived at the drive-in, parked, got all our snacks, and settled in for the movie, my dad told me to come sit up front with him in the driver's seat. I rushed up to the front as if I had won a prize.

As the movie progressed, I realized that the only prize I won was being in arm's reach so he could cover my eyes during the nasty parts of the movie. Yeah, that was a smooth move on his part. I'll remember next time to decline his offer.

II. First Rehab (Age 13)

Today my aunt came to pick me up. A few choice family members were going up in the mountains to see my dad at some rehab place. The night before I asked my mom if I had to go, and she said I didn't, but she knew it would mean a lot to dad to see me and it might make a big difference in his life. Well gee, Mom, with that kind of pressure, I soon found myself in the car listening to a conversation

48

that I thought was pure nonsense. To be honest, I really didn't know them (his family) that well. I wasn't around much.

But as we got closer to this place, I got butterflies in the pit of my stomach, because my dad, this man, had not been a part of my life, yet everyone was acting like I was the center of his. How could that be? I didn't know how I was supposed to act or what to say.

We finally got there. I felt nothing familiar. My impression was that he didn't look as bad as addicts do, but he didn't look too well kept either. Recovery, I guess.

I didn't talk much, spoke when spoken to, answered questions when asked. The final act was the good-bye hug. I'm pretty sure he said he loved me, and I probably said it back as a courteous response. We had no relationship.

I was glad to be getting closer to the car. I felt more relaxed. I couldn't wait to get back home, get back to what I knew, where I went to sleep and woke up. Maybe I'd pick on my lil' sisters, the secret love language of siblings. That is, if my older brother didn't get to me first (the secret language of older brothers).

III. Clothing Store (Age 19)

Today while shopping for my own inappropriate clothing to go out dancing, a nearby conversation caught my attention. A young girl was debating with her father, arguing her case that the skirt she wanted wasn't too short. (Actually it was, but she wasn't that much younger than me.)

At first I smiled, thankful that I didn't have to deal with such drama. But as I moved around the rack, my smile disappeared, and so did my thankful attitude. I listened as "the father" gave his daughter the short version of "a woman's appearance and a man's perception of that appearance." She listened, but I could tell by her facial expression that her priority was the skirt.

Eventually they came to a compromise, and I just stood there for a minute after they left, wondering where my father figure was. Where was the man who would keep me from falling into the traps of men? Well, whatever, I thought. I was still going to the party.

IV. Poem: Who Are You? (Age 24)

What can you say
About a man you never knew
A man who never showed up
For birthday parities

Never saw report cards
Never met you at the corner
For the walk home from school

A man who wasn't there
For the toothaches or the
Late-night coughing spells
A man who made you number six
On his top-five list
Of drugs and alcohol

One who couldn't possibly
Understand
The meaning of parental sacrifice
The abandonment of pride or
The things one does to ensure
His kids are clothed and fed

A man who has no clue
Who is the woman he helped create
A man
Some would describe as father
Is a man I will never know

Life is hard in a single-parent home
The sacrifices are greater
The space is more confined
But the bond from surviving
The struggle
Is immeasurable

What can you say
About a man you never knew

Absolutely Nothing

Tiffaney
May 25, 1999

I was too selfish to stop getting high and live the "one-time-only experience" of watching my daughter grow up to become the woman she is today. Too selfish to take a hand in shaping the character she will instill in her (my) future through her (my) children (grandchildren). Cunning, baffling, and powerful. This came to me about my daughter:

Poem to My Daughter

The time has come, the day finally arrived
By the facts and the figure the truth can no longer hide
I've always known it was coming; boy it's true what they say
She's always been your little girl, then you notice one day
When you look at her now, the little girl has gone away
What you see now is like the beginning of a flower
That will blossom and bloom in all its colorful power
A chapter is closing on her little girl ways
One is beginning on her young woman days
My girl was pretty in a childlike sort of way
But now she's brown and lovely, and kind of curvy, I might say
Too much time with the little girl was missed
Though no fault of hers, let me tell you this
I love you, Tiffaney, and *God* knows this is true
I love you and I pray to be a better father to you
The years flew by so fast, and I haven't seen you that much
Because all I did was keep in touch
You are more important to me than you'll ever know
But I know I have to do more than say it; I'll have to show
And show it I will, because I have the faith

In *God*, in His wisdom, His mercy, and His grace
Yes, now you're a young woman lovely and smart
Always in my thoughts and also in my heart
Since you were a baby, till you're old and gray
In my heart you'll always be my baby girl, until my dying day

No one can really appreciate how grateful, how truly thankful, a recovering alcoholic/addict is unless he too has been delivered from seemingly complete hopelessness by a Higher Power.

16

The Gift

Though you might look free, you are a complete slave to the spirit of your drug of choice.

In May 1990, my son was shot and then dragged a few blocks under a car in a drive-by shooting. I received a call that night from my mother informing me that Eddie Jr. had been shot. She'd been told that he was dead and was lying in the middle of the street by his mother's house. When I got the call, I was lying on the bed thinking about how I could come up with some money for dope in the morning.

I jumped up and threw on some clothes and was soon out the door to find out what had happened. By the time I got out to the car, my disease had come up with a new plan: get some dope for the morning. All I had to do was go by the dope man's house first, on the way to see what had happened to my son. I was a good customer and an excellent liar when the need arose. The way I reasoned it, if Eddie Jr. was dead, I couldn't help him now anyway.

I know he had tried to reach me all day, and the day before, but I just thought he wanted some money, so I didn't try to call him back. Well, anyway, it was too late now. But if I played it right, I could get some dope out of the killing.

I entered the dope man's house visibly shaken; everybody could see it. I made my legs shake just enough to make my gait seem unsteady. When I reached for the chair and the table to sit down, my hands had just the right tremor to them. My voice was broken and strained with just the right pitch. My eyes had that vacant, faraway look, and I just stared at the table. I hardly made eye contact with anyone in the room.

"Man, what's wrong?" they said.

"My-my-my son has just been killed," I whimpered, keeping my eyes on the floor and shaking my head in disbelief, for effect.

"What!" everybody in the house said in unison, and I went on to give the gory details, although I knew only what my mother had told me over the phone. Oh, but I was good! I told them about the bloody bullet holes, the gory rips and tears from being dragged under a car through the streets, the bone-shattering climax as the shooters ran over him to make their getaway.

As I told the story, I kept my eyes glued to the table, my voice barely audible. They had to pay attention to hear me. I wanted to make sure everyone heard. I wanted all of their sympathy, in case they had to take a collection to buy me some dope. I tried to cover all angles. When I finished telling the tale, you could hear a pin drop anywhere in the house.

I finished and straightened up and looked the dope man in the eye. I said, "Look, man, it's going to be a long night. I'm going to have to go over there and make positive ID. I don't want to. My wife can't. She won't believe it's him until I tell her it is. He's my son. It's up to me to do it." Now I was staring at the table again.

Straightening up again and looking at him again, I said, "Man, I need a bag of dope to get me through. You know death means money to the family. We had insurance. I'll pay you tomorrow, definitely by the next day."

"Damn, Ed, I'm sorry to hear that. Yeah, man, of course. I'll give you two bags. That way you'll have one for your morning wakeup," he said.

"Thanks, man," I said, showing him a fake weak smile. Inside I was singing and shouting, *Oh, Happy Day.*

Since I was in such a shaken state, I decided to fix one bag of dope quick—you know, because of my distraught condition. I easily convinced myself that I needed a shot of medicine before I made my fateful drive. I felt good as I left the dope house on my way to where my son was supposed to be lying. I felt even better knowing I had a bag of dope for later on. Like I said, if he was dead, wasn't nothing I could do anyhow. Might as well get me some dope out of it.

I made my way over to the alleged scene of the crime. I got caught by a couple of stoplights on my way over there. I nodded a little bit each time I waited for the light to change. Man, that was some good dope.

When I got to my ex-wife's house, there was a big crowd on the far corner. I got out of the car and neared the crowd. I could hear some youngsters saying, "Man, they got Ed. Ed2's been shot. He's dead."

I made my way over to the police barricade and went under the yellow tape. I was stopped by an officer as I made my way to where a group of policemen were standing.

"This is a crime scene area. You have to get back on the other side of the barricade," the officer said.

"I was told my son may be the one who's lying over there."

"What's your name?"

I told him.

"You got some ID?"

I showed him.

The officer looked over my ID then handed it back to me.

"We're pretty sure it's him. There was a female with him. She wasn't shot, but she was run over too. She has a broken leg. Your son, well, he was shot a number of times. He fell in front of the car and was run over with the girl. He was caught under the car and dragged quite a distance."

"Is he dead?"

"Yeah, there's a good chance he died from the gunshots before he hit the ground. I hope he wasn't alive when they dragged him," he said.

"Where is he?" I said, looking in the direction of the group of police officers.

"This is a crime scene and nobody is supposed to come through. But if you really insist, I won't stop you. I'm a father, too. I got a teenage son. This is from one father to another. I've seen your son. The car really messed him up. Believe me, you'd do better to remember what your son looked like the last time you saw him. If you go over there and look at what's lying on the ground, you'll never forget what your son looked like the last time you saw him. You don't want to remember him like that. You'd never forget it. I know I won't."

I was watching his face as he spoke to me. His eyes didn't lie. They held compassion. For that moment, we were just two fathers. He wanted to spare me, spare me from the vision I would have to endure for a lifetime if I looked. I decided to trust the officer's advice. I decided to remember my son as I had last seen him alive. I wouldn't look at the disfigured remains in the street. Besides, if I settled on this rationale, I wouldn't have to admit to myself that looking at his dead, torn up body might bring down my high.

Again, in hindsight, too late did I realize the precious gift I had been given. I am now painfully aware of the gift I lost. The *God* of my understanding gave me this about my son:

The Gift

A child is a gift sent from above

To be treated with kindness, showered with love

A child is a gift that grows every day

Learning to live, to find its own way

A child is a loan, and the interest is high

You'll continue to pay till the day that you die
A child is joy, a child is sorrow
They'll always surprise you, just wait till tomorrow
A child is a statement of what you believe
They'll either have morals or do as they please
A child is always with you, even when they're not there
Seems the more you put in, the less that they care
Your child is your bounty, your child fills a need
Your child is the future, bearer of your seed
My gift was a son from my *Father* above
And though I loved him true, in truth did I love?
My gift is gone, no longer here
I realize how precious, I realize how dear
When the time is right in the *Master's* Plan
I know I'll join him and walk hand in hand

When you're hooked on alcohol and drugs, the longer you're in bondage to addiction, the more immune you become to feelings for anyone, especially those close to you. All cares are stripped away, except one. You care only for drugs and alcohol. There's nothing left for anything or anyone. Putting this on paper—pulling thoughts from inside and writing them down, looking at what is inside, what I've kept hidden from view for so long—is painful. My eyes start to tear as I'm writing this down. I have to stop and keep wiping them. I don't want anyone walking in on me and catching me crying. Hey! Recovery is about change—change from inside out. I realize crying is nothing to be ashamed of. I'm glad I'm beginning to feel things inside. Monsters don't feel things inside, do they?

I feel good and sad at the same time. Sad because I've missed so much of the growing up time of my family. Sad because I know I've squandered the most priceless commodities in the universe, my health and my youth, on alcohol and drugs. Sad because I can never tell my son, Eddie I'm sorry, I love you, give me a chance to make it right.

But I feel good too. Maybe this is what they mean when they say "tears of joy." I feel good because I'm no longer in bondage to addiction, feel good that I'm free from alcohol and drugs, feel good that I'm no longer afraid to face life as it comes.

17

A Real Man

I feel good because I've found a Power that delivered me and will keep me as long as I trust Him and believe He is able. I feel good because I can finally begin to be what I should have been all along, a real man. This is what I now believe a real man is:

A Real Man

Growing up little did I realize or begin to understand

The sacrifice, ingratitude, the love-hate attributes of being a real man?

Dad's feelings for me seemed to change with each year that I grew

From "You're always Daddy's baby" to "Child, what is wrong with you?"

From piggy-back

To no, you can't do that

From always having fun

To no, not until your work is done

From "You're Daddy's pretty girl" to "Oh no. That boy's no good for you"

Or "Son, I got college plans for you. You and that girl are through"

Most times I would love him; most times I'd hate him too

I just didn't know any better, what a real man must go through

Didn't know that a real man was a hero, not like the comics because
he is flesh and blood

A real man has to wear many hats, but more important, he gets his
direction from above

It's not easy to always do what's right; it's so much easier to do what's
wrong

But a Spirit-filled *Christ*-directed father has no choice; for family's
sake he must be strong

Food, clothes, shelter are just the basics, not for just a day but for
years that see no end

Projected years of sacrificing and saving for others when that money
could have been used for good timing with friends

You didn't have no car when you were still wet behind the ears, so
why get one for them

Because *Christ* made you a father and blessed you with gifts of love
that came directly from *Him*

A real man will work those extra hours at the job and then come
home and work some more

Buy new school clothes for his kids while he stands around looking
poor

A real man can love you then tell you no, when he knows you'll hate
his guts

Turn right around and give you words of encouragement when he
sees you're in a rut

The *Lord* said, "Greater love hath no man than this, that he lay down
his life for another"

A real man gives of his life every day for his wife, his kids, or a fellow
Christian brother

A real man knows he's a caretaker for his Master *Jesus Christ*

Entrusted to guide his family home, to be with the real *Father*
through Eternal Life

I'm glad *God* blessed me to be born a male, even though I'm just now beginning to understand what it is to be a man. Most males believe that if you are born

male and live long enough, you automatically become a man. I once believed this too. But it's not true: some males never become men no matter how old they become. Why do most women know this fact of life early on? (Anyway, that's another story.)

Becoming a real man, like anything else, takes instruction, practice, and prayer. Unfortunately, many youth in America today, especially ethnic youth, have far too few role models in this area.

Let me also say this: I said I felt blessed that *God* made me a male. I am. But I was in no way implying that if you were born a woman you weren't blessed. To the contrary, *God* said, "It is not good for man to be alone. I will make him a helper suitable for him." That is a spiritual truth straight out of the mouth of the Creator. A man is not complete without a woman. He is not whole and cannot function to fullness.

Take the example of a brand-new car, shiny and sleek. A powerfully built engine, new rubber all the way around, ready to go. But there's no gas in it. Without gas, all it can do is sit there. While it's sitting there, it might look good. But without the gas, it can't do what it was made to do, run. The birds might sit on it, or someone else might sit in it, as it's just sitting there, but that's not its function. The car needs the gas to be whole and to function as it was meant to.

A real man needs a woman to be whole. What better example could an infinite, loving *God* give to man than to show him the capacity to love through his woman? Most males never realize the powerful gift their women have the capacity to bestow. A real man is forever amazed by the depth of his woman's love and will emulate her example for his family.

18

Mom

I've always had an example of that type of love right in front of me. But like most males, I'd always look but never see. My mother and grandmother steadfastly prayed for me throughout my addiction, always believing *God* was able to help me and praying for his will. This is what *God* gave me about my mother:

Mom

Just a few lines could never describe
The enormity of your meaning to me, but in these few I've
Glimpsed a small measure of that bounty which is your Love
From my first remembrance you've been my source
I've drawn from you
Like the deepest well, your love for me never dried up
Even when I should have been unlovable, even when I betrayed you
Even when I hurt you
You loved me still, and in my heart I know you always will
It's a blessing from *God* to have a Mother's Love
While she's on earth—and when she's above
You're a part of her and you'll always be
Her love will never leave you, and it's forever free

What better example of selfless love than a mother's love for her child? What won't she sacrifice or do for the betterment of her child? How much greater is your God's, your Creator's, Love for you. What won't He do for you if you would only let Him?

19

Who's Really to Blame?

With hindsight, I can see my past with greater clarity: The times I thought I should have died. The times I should have gone to jail. The people I've hurt that didn't hurt me back. I could say I've been very lucky. But today I don't believe in luck. I've been blessed. I was blessed when I didn't deserve it. I've been shown unmerited favor.

But at the time I was always complaining, always blaming, always making excuses. It was always somebody else's fault. As I pondered these things, *God* showed me who was really to blame:

Who's Really to Blame?

Who can I point the finger at? Who's really to blame?

Someone else has to be the cause of the wreckage and insanity my life has claimed

Could have been my parents—they didn't love or treat me right

Or that uncle or aunt or brother or sister that didn't do the right thing when they tucked me in at night

Maybe it was the kids who used to tease me, called me fat, ugly, skinny, or black

The kids who never wanted to be my friend, just find something about me to attack

It might have been that first boy or girl on whom you had a crush

That would laugh along with all the rest, look at you and turn away in disgust

Could have been that guy you thought really loved you, but just used
    you, laughed and then told everybody you weren't the best
Or that girl you knew loved only you, till you learned you were just a
    number, just like the rest
Blame it on the ones with you, when peer pressure made you take
    that first drink
Somebody messed up your life; the name's on the tip of your
    tongue—just think

Someone is the reason your life turned out the way it did
Someone is the reason all my opportunities eventually hit the skids
It's not my fault all my relationships fell apart
I'm not to blame; I'm alone, with no one to share my heart

I know my drinking is not to blame—alcohol's been my only true
    friend
Looking at the wreckage of my past, only alcohol's stuck it out with
    me to the bitter end
When job's fell through and friends went away, only alcohol could
    soothe the pain that came my way
When the love grew cold, it was because of the other; that's what I
    would always say

Only my friend alcohol could get me through those days
When others did, only alcohol wouldn't reject me
Yes, others were to blame for the state my life was in
Alcohol had always been there, loved me through thick and thin

One day I met a man who said he could relate to all I was saying
Said he'd been just like me, but no longer misery for life was he
    paying
Said he'd been introduced to a way, and just twelve steps it would
    take
To realize who was to blame for all my misery and my life's heartache

I found that way and took those steps and learned what he had said
    was true
Learned I was powerless, that my life was unmanageable, but there
    was something else to do
Turn my life and my will over to God, as I understood Him
And I realized I'm responsible, and only I deserved the blame that I
    always gave to them

No longer covered by the blanket of denial, I could see that I had caused myself much grief over the years, with the deviations I had taken and the decisions I had made—decisions influenced by the disease of addiction, which put me deeper and deeper into the debt of misery and despair. They compounded daily, year after year, and I was quickly spiritually bankrupt.

A life of living forfeited to mere existence in bondage. A slave to alcohol and drugs, my Master the Spirit of Addiction. And like a slave, I developed a slave's mentality. Not wanting to escape, not believing anything was better, accepting that this was the way it was supposed to be.

But like most Evil Masters, they always want more, never satisfied with what you've already done. They will treat you worse and worse, always taking more and more from you day after day, year after year, until you finally have nothing left to give. You have to decide if you're going to stay under that Master and die, or rise up and seek to live.

20

Chosen One

Many alcoholics and addicts are thick-skinned and hardheaded. They have to be whipped by an existence in bondage for a long time before they can shout, "Stop! I want to live. Please, *God*, help me." Some never say it and seal their fate. I'm glad *God* made me one of the Chosen Ones:

Chosen One

It's humbling and at the same time amusing for those blessed to have lived through

The chaos and wreckage of their past when feeling sad, getting mad, and causing pain was all we knew how to do

Good times and bad, feeling sorrow, being glad. Just look at me. I was having fun

But more and more despair behind the happy face I'd wear, spirit numb, for I knew I was an Unlucky One

Being the life of the party for all to see

No one knew, though we looked alike, it wasn't me

The look-alike would drink and use all night long and greet the sun

The look-alike would do it, because he knew I was an Unlucky One

I can look back at the time and remember, I could work the job and not think about a drink

I can look back at the time and remember when all through the job of alcohol I'd stink

I can look back at the time when I'd blame the boss, my co-workers,
   or the pressure from being under the gun
I can look back at the time and remember, I said I couldn't hold a
   job, because I was an Unlucky One

My family didn't understand me; they were mean, they abused, and
   molested me too
Nightmares, painful memories. I know no one can relate—well
   maybe just a few of you
I took the drink and used the drugs to forget, but when all was said
   and done
Deep down I knew all these things were happening to me because I
   was just an Unlucky One

I didn't want to drink or use, but the look-alike said life would be too
   dull
I couldn't handle or take care of anything; my life had become
   unmanageable
Crushing was the weight of misery in my life; if measured by the
   pound, I had a ton
Why, *God*, why me, why am I just one of the Unlucky Ones

My so-called life of abusing had become a treadmill, always turning,
   and I had no power to make it stop
Jails, institutions, or death waited for me; the production of my life
   was a flop
I wanted it over, I couldn't live and wouldn't die, I realized from
   myself I couldn't outrun
Fate had put its mark on me and made me one of the Unlucky Ones

Yes, I remember all of that, remember it exactly ten years ago
   yesterday
Remember the man who introduced me to another way of life he
   called the AA way

Introduced me to the Twelve Steps, being powerless, surrendering,
  turning over your will, and how a new life is begun
I began to learn that I was not unlucky, but that I was a Chosen One

Nothing happens in *God's* world by accident; I truly believe I'm
  exactly where I should be, right now, today
I'm not a normie; I'm an alcoholic/addict, and just for today, I
  wouldn't have it any other way
Finally, I've learned to live through One who is greater than me,
  learned on a daily basis how my life's battles can be won
I thank my *Higher Power*, the *God* of my understanding, that *He*
  blessed me to be one of the *Chosen Ones*

In Hebrews 12:6–11, it states that if *God* accepts you as one of His own, one of His children, then just like a loving human father, He will discipline his child when he sees him going astray. Your Heavenly Father will lovingly allow you to command your own ship, even if you run yourself aground time and time again. He will allow you to try every way you can, to do it your way.

Then, when you finally humble yourself and admit your way is no way, when you honestly call out to Him from your heart, He will be there for you, as He has been all along. He knows what is best. His way is the right way. He can see farther down the road than you can. He knows what obstacles are in front of you, which ones you should avoid and which ones will make you stronger. Let Him guide you, for it is His road. Trust and believe that your *God* is able.

For over thirty years, I was determined to do things my way, to run my own show. At times during those years, things were sweet. I knew I had my life on course. But time after time, I would wreck on some unforeseen rock in the water. My ship would go down again.

My *God* would let me use the brush of despair and hopelessness to paint myself into life's corner. The best thing I ever did in my forty-five years of life was to surrender in my heart and cry out to *God* for help, to admit I was powerless over drugs and alcohol and powerless to run my own life. I asked the *God* of my own understanding to take over; I would follow His lead. I gave Him my addiction, asked Him to keep it because I couldn't handle it.

It's been a little over ten years, and I haven't asked Him to give it back, thinking I could handle it. The *God* I serve will lovingly give me back my addiction if I feel I need one more lesson in that ill-fated course: *How to Handle Drugs and Alcohol Addiction Yourself 101.*

21

What's His Name

Cunning, baffling, and powerful, the disease of addiction will forever wait for me to get from behind the protection of my New Sovereign and Lord. The disease of addiction has and will beat me by myself every time. I've got a new Master, a *God* of my own understanding who has my best interest at heart. He's been here forever, but I never knew Him. We've just been introduced. Let me give you the name of the *God* of my understanding:

What's His Name

Jesus, Jesus, that's His name
Ask me again, yeah, I'll tell you the same
I'll tell you He not only died on Calvary
I'll tell you what He did for me
I'll tell you how I was doomed through dope
Tell you how I found true hope
Ask me how I lied and lived to steal
How for me, to the Father, He made an appeal
For dope I ran the night to and fro
Through Jesus now, I don't have to go
My life's not perfect, I still have fears
But instead of dope, I keep Jesus near
He promised to be with me, never leave me alone
Whenever I call Him, He's always home
If my path gets rocky or I start to stray
I can call on Jesus to show me the way
Jesus, Jesus, that's His name

Ask me again, yeah, I'll tell you the same
He died for you, and He died for me
You can have life, you can be free
If you're bound by drugs—whatever—it's still sin
Accept the Lord as your Savior, be born again
Yeah, Jesus, Jesus, is His name
Ask me again and I'll tell you the same

Yes, *Jesus* is the name of my *Higher Power*. Through Jesus I receive power to affect change in my life. For me, it is extremely important to identify the *Higher Power* that I'm calling out to for help.

For a few years, I was deeply involved in the occult. In the practice of the dark arts, you are instructed to call on entities that dwell in the spiritual realm by name for power and insight. These entities are real and have power, and in the 90s they were as close as your nearest psychic hotline. The seemingly benevolent help psychics offer humans does not come without a satanic catch. Simply picking up the phone and calling on the spiritual realm—and not identifying who you want your help to come from—may cost you more than you intended to pay.

My twelve-step program was a spiritual program designed to spiritually effect a change in my physical behavior. Just as all things on the physical plane are not good for us, not everything in the spiritual realm is good for us. Satan and his demons are in the spiritual realm (Ephesians 6:12). Typically, most of us know (or care) much less about the spiritual world than we do about the material world.

When working with a spiritual twelve-step program and seeking help to change from a *God* that is spiritual, doesn't it make sense to look for guidance in a book that has knowledge about the spiritual realm?

Personally, I choose the *Bible*. The twelve-step program does not tell you which *God* to choose as your *Higher Power*. But choose a *Higher Power* you must to effect real change (repentance) in your life. The God I chose, or rather accepted, the God of my understanding, left sixty-six books describing His person, the spirit realm, earth, me, and how I can have power and abundant life through His Son, *Jesus Christ*.

It was my choice. I chose.

The result was that after thirty years of drinking and using drugs, I'm no longer in bondage to the Spirit of Addiction. I can't say I have arrived yet and that my life is now perfect. On the contrary, now I'm just average, like everybody else, trying to live life on life's terms. No, I still have character defects.

But after thirty years, I'm free. The unbearable weight of addiction has been lifted off of me. The ball and chain of alcohol and drugs have been loosed from my spirit. My emotional and spiritual growth can commence after being stunted thirty years. Finally, with Jesus in the crow's nest, I know my ship is on the right course.

22

Epilog

People use all types of gauges to measure success—power, money, sexual conquest, beauty, determination, inner peace, strength, health—you name it and somebody somewhere is swearing how successful they are at it. For the greater portion of my life, success has been a foreign term, outside my realm of reality. Not being an alcoholic or a dope addict is normal for most people and wouldn't rate high on their gauge of success. But for a person addicted to anything who has been blessed to overcome his addiction, the words "normal" and "average" take on whole new meanings.

My perception and reaction to external stimuli (life) has been changed. I've lived abnormally for so long that I welcome normalcy as the blessing it really is. My parents trust me again. They no longer rush to put their valuables under lock and key when they see me coming.

My daughter told me she's proud of me. She said she was glad I was her father. Only a parent who has lost the love and respect of his child and then been given an opportunity to earn back that love and respect can know the enormity of those few words: "I'm glad you are my father."

I've gone back to school and earned an Associate of Arts degree in Psychology with a Certificate of Completion in Substance Abuse. I then continued on, earning a Bachelor of Arts degree in Social Work from Cal State Los Angeles. I then completed a master's degree in Social Work on a California State University campus.

I've discovered that I like to write, and I have become an avid writer and poet. I believe in a *God* that knows I'm alive. I've finally tasted success with the things I've just named. My life is full of expectations, because every day I am that much further from the old me and that much further into the new me.

Whatever is taking place in my life, I know that my *God* is able. He's shown me what He can do in my life. I believe and trust Him to guide me through whatever life I have left. This is my tenth year without a puff of smoke (weed, tobacco, or cocaine); a sip of beer, wine, or whiskey; or a shot of heroin into my arm. My tenth year following the *God* (Jesus Christ) of my understanding.

I must say, it's been a totally different experience from what I've been used to. Things have been pretty good. No, contrary to popular belief, when you begin to trust in Jesus, everything doesn't become perfect, everything doesn't fall right into place, everyone doesn't immediately begin to love you and think you're great. Overall, I think what I've gotten most out of these post-addiction years is the feeling of being at ease, a feeling of peace. No matter what the circumstances, whether I deem them good or bad, *Jesus* is in control of my life. Whatever happens, with *Jesus*, it will be all right.

Ed Houston
8-20-04

23

Postscript

PS:

This is something I had to share with you. Out of everything, it is the most important thing to me, and it validates everything I've said before. It's from my daughter. This is the letter she wrote to me this last Father's Day. God is so good.

It never seems to be the right time to break out in this big, emotional declaration of love. But then, at the same time, how quickly we regret the things never said when the ones we love don't see tomorrow. I know you know that *I love you*, because I tell you with my own mouth and mean it with all my heart. Yet, every time I see you, there is so much more that I want you to know. There should be no question in your mind of how extremely proud I am of you. I am so thankful that you never gave up on me, and I know that may sound backwards, but if you had not pursued a relationship with me, there wouldn't be one. And I would be missing out on something I never thought I wanted or needed.

My mom has never spoken against you or provided information on the things she went through. The stories I do know, you've told me with great remorse. Even on that issue, all that comes to mind is, *What an improvement, look at you now!* You have *God* in your life, and it shows. You're a husband, a college grad, a good father, an even better grandpa to Jazlynn and, if you ask Marlisa or Nurisha, the greatest uncle ever. I am so proud of you, proud you are my dad. I brag about you. I miss you when I don't see or talk to you, and I enjoy calling you for no reason at all. I love the fact that you understand that I am a wife and mother and that my time is not always available. A lot of people don't get that. I thank *God* that *He* gave you the strength and determination to turn your life completely around and kept you moving forward. I know it was worth it for you, but it also benefited me. I never thought I needed you in my life, and you'll never know how grateful I am that you proved me wrong.

Your ever-loving daughter
Tiff
Father's Day
June 2004

Do I need to say anything else other than "Thank you, Jesus!" I think not.

978-0-595-39641-2
0-595-39641-0

Printed in the United States
79674LV00005B/598-627